ON THE WATER!

Written by **Claire Philip**
Illustrated by **Ailie Busby**

WINDMILL BOOKS
™

Published in 2023 by Windmill Books,
an Imprint of Rosen Publishing
2544 Clinton St.
Buffalo, NY 14224

Copyright © 2021 by Miles Kelly Publishing

Cataloging-in-Publication Data

Names: Philip, Claire, author. | Busby, Ailie, illustrator.
Title: On the water! / by Claire Philip, illustrated by Ailie Busby.
Description: New York : Windmill Books, 2023. | Series: On the go!
Identifiers: ISBN 9781538392799 (pbk.) | ISBN 9781538392805 (library bound) | ISBN 9781538392812 (ebook)
Subjects: LCSH: Boats and boating--Pictorial works--Juvenile literature. | Ships--Pictorial works--Juvenile literature.
Classification: LCC GV775.3 P455 2023 | DDC 799.1--dc23

Printed in the United States of America

CPSIA Compliance Information: Batch #CWWM23
For Further Information contact Rosen Publishing at 1-800-237-9932

Find us on

Making a splash

Most of our planet is covered in water.
We splash our way across it in ships,
boats, and other kinds of watercraft.

Speedboat

Water skis

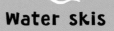

Windsurfing
board

Woof
Woof!

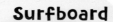

Surfboard

This large boat is a **passenger ferry**. Its job is to carry people, and sometimes cars, across the sea.

Go left!

Jet Skis are super fast, so they are perfect for towing wakeboards.

Some people fish or do yoga on their paddleboards!

Kiteboard

Paddleboard

3

Paddle time!

Many types of boats can be propelled through the water using people power!

I'm made from a hollowed-out tree.

Rowboat

Wooden raft

I'm going to catch fish for dinner!

Reed boat

Dugout

Coracle

All watercraft, even the simplest boats, have a watertight body called a **hull**.

Paddles and oars are used to propel a kayak through the water.

Canoe

Look out ahead!

Inflatable kayak

5

Super sails

Sailboats and sailing ships are powered by the wind, which is captured using sails.

Sloop

Mast

I move quickly through the waves!

Catamaran

Sails are large pieces of cloth that are attached to a mast.

I'm the most common kind of sailboat!

Yawl

Keel

Need for speed

Trimarans are boats with three hulls instead of one.

There's the finish line!

Due to their design, trimarans are very difficult to sink! They can stay upright even in the worst storms.

As the main hull is narrow, there isn't much room inside the cabin.

We don't need much wind to sail!

Trimarans are easier to control than boats, so they are often used in racing.

Whoosh!

Engine Power

Not all boats have sails. Motorboats have an engine that sits inside the boat or at its rear.

Bowriders are used for water sports and for cruising the open water.

A **cabin cruiser** is perfect for a vacation on the water. Most have places to cook and sleep.

Riding on air

Hovercraft can travel across land and water.

Propellers at the back of the hovercraft push it forward.

Fans fill the area underneath the craft, called the **skirt**, with air. This lifts it off the ground.

Living on board

People also buy or build boats to use as homes as well as transportation.

More than 10,000 people live on **houseboats** on the River Thames in London in the United Kingdom.

Good morning!

Canals are human-made waterways. They were once important travel routes. Today, people live or vacation on canal boats.

Beautiful **houseboats** are found in Kerala, in India. In the past, they were used as transportation, and for carrying rice and spices.

Amsterdam, in the Netherlands, is famous for the colorful houseboats on its canals.

city of water

The Italian city of Venice is made up of more than 100 islands and almost 200 canals.

Vaporettos are a kind of motorboat used as public transportation instead of buses.

All shapes and sizes

Big, small, fast, slow – there's a whole world of weird and wonderful watercraft!

Tanker ship

Tugboat

Super yacht

I take people on luxury trips!

Airboat

Steamboat

I am powered by steam!

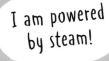

Dragon boat

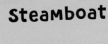

Pedal boat

Sampan boat

Iceboat

At high speeds, I lift out of the water!

Whitewater raft

Hydrofoil

Drillship

19

A trip on a ship

Cruise ships are like floating hotels! They can be enormous, with lots of cabins for people to sleep in.

The biggest have restaurants, pools, gyms – even theaters!

Next stop, Alaska!

Some cruise ships sail the seas, while smaller versions float along rivers.

They are usually painted white.

The biggest cruise ships can carry more than 5,000 passengers!

Cruise ships take people on **tours**. This means they stop at lots of different places, giving people a chance to explore.

21

Working ships

If you want to move lots of things a long way, or battle through icy waters, you'll need a really massive ship!

ILK 610-23

A container ship moves cargo in large boxes called containers.

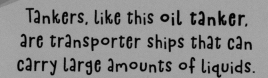

Tankers, like this oil tanker, are transporter ships that can carry large amounts of liquids.

Bulk carriers move huge quantities of goods, such as coal or grain, but they are loose and not in containers.

I'm carrying tons of coal!

Aircraft carriers have a runway on board so that planes can take off at sea!

Icebreaker ships are used to push through large sheets of ice so that other ships and boats can get through.

Diving deep

Submarines and submersibles are vessels that can sink beneath the waves.

Submarines can carry many people on board. They are used for exploring and traveling deep below the water's surface.

Submersibles can reach the ocean floor. Scientists use them to study deep-sea creatures.

That's a strange fish!